MW00883770

A Time for Choosing

A Christian Declaration on the Value of Human Life

Peter Heck

Library of Congress Cataloging-in-Publication Data

ISBN-13: 978-1983441219
ISBN-10: 198344121X

Published in the United States by
Attaboy Press

a division of Attaboy Productions, Inc.
2139 Emily Court
Kokomo, IN 46902

For more information on Attaboy Productions, Inc., please visit:
www.peterheck.com

Distributed in cooperation with
CreateSpace
7290 B. Investment Drive
Charleston, SC 29418

To Mike and Dave, the most dedicated servants
to this cause I've ever met.

CONTENTS

1

DEFINING MOMENTS

I remember it like it was yesterday. Playing in the front yard of our home in Terre Haute, Indiana with my older brother when we heard the sound of a car pulling in the long driveway. We turned around to see exactly what we were waiting for all morning. My Dad was returning from his month-long tour of duty with the United States Air Force.

We were always excited when Dad came home from these kinds of trips not just because we'd missed him, but because he would always bring back some sort of gift for us. It was never anything big, but a surprise nonetheless.

And sure enough, after he and mom became reacquainted when he got out of the car (something that no preteen child wants to see), he reached in the backseat and pulled out two large brown paper sacks and told us to head inside because he got us something.

Since Andrew was older, he got to open his first. Excitedly, he tore into it and pulled out a brand new, NFL regulation-size football. He wanted to run straight to the phone to call up all the neighborhood kids to come play, but before he did that, it was my turn. With great anticipation I ripped my bag open and pulled out a brand new, dark-skinned, blond-haired Barbie doll named PJ.

And if you're tempted to think that the sad part of this story is imagining my poor dad having to take those two items to the store clerk for purchase and explain that these weren't gifts for his son and daughter, but his son...and other son...it's actually worse. Everyone in my family can attest to the fact that based on reactions to the presents, I was far more excited about getting PJ than Andrew was about getting the football.

That evening as I sat in my room changing her from evening wear to swimwear, my open window allowed me to hear the sounds of the neighborhood boys all over playing football in the front yard. Amidst a pile of Barbie clothes that evening, I realized something: I was at a defining moment in my life. I was going to decide that night whether for the rest of my life I was going to be a football guy ... or a Barbie guy.

I thank God for the decision I made that night to lay down my Barbies. And other than a few brief moments of weakness, I assure you, I haven't played with them since.

We talk about defining moments all the time – those moments when decisions we make alter the course and direction of our lives...the life of our family, church, community, culture, country, or even our civilization.

Perhaps no other issue defines a people

more clearly, more completely, more lucidly, than the dignity and respect they show to human life. Beyond economics and education, laws and literature, show me the regard they collectively hold for the sanctity of human life, and I will show you their ultimate destiny.

That's why I always found it odd when I used to talk about the sanctity of life (manifesting in issues like abortion, infanticide, euthanasia, suicide, doctor-assisted suicide) on the radio and would face strong pushback from listeners lecturing me that there are "more important things to talk about." Really? Like what?

I'm not being obtuse or argumentative with that question. I'm being serious. If the issue of life and death, and the value we place on the human experience as a society is not the most important, most pressing, most critical issue there is to discuss, what is? For all the times I asked it, I never got an answer. There's a reason for that.

But I'm going to assume since you picked up this book, you already know all this. I'm going to assume I don't need to spend an inordinate amount of your time telling you why these debates about life and death are the most serious we face. I'm going to assume that what you're looking for is not an answer to the question why is this important but rather what can I do?

I think I can answer that for you.

2

STOP WAITING ON POLITICIANS

The hardest thing for someone like me (and maybe someone like you) to accept about issues involving the value and sanctity of human life is that they can't be decided at the ballot box. Don't get me wrong, there is certainly a morally correct position to take when it comes to legislation involving abortion, euthanasia, and suicide. And Christians shouldn't be afraid to speak out for that morally correct position.

But if we want to be effective, we also have to be realistic. Other than a handful of elected officials, politicians will *follow* the masses rather than *lead* the masses. It's a pretty simple formula for them:

2. Stop Waiting on Politicians

Majority of voters hold position A

If they venture too far from position A, they will lose their job to someone holding position A

Thus, they will not venture far from position A

If position A is some morally incoherent, intellectually inconsistent philosophy, we can (and should) acknowledge that and rebuke it. But we also have to expect that our politicians will not stray from it because it's not politically expedient for them to do so. Until the culture is persuaded to shamefully correct and move past position A, politicians who want to remain employed will accept it (outright or by default) regardless of how heinous it is.

A few examples might help illustrate this point.

1. In December of 2002, Scott Peterson murdered his wife Laci and their unborn son Conner in Modesto, California. Peterson wanted to escape his marriage and upcoming

parenthood, and had started having an affair with a massage therapist named Amber Frey shortly before the slayings.

After the bodies of both Laci and Conner washed up on the shore of the San Francisco Bay in April of 2003, Peterson was arrested and went to trial. Despite pleading not guilty, a 12-person jury found him guilty of first and second-degree murder. He was later sentenced to death for his crimes.

Just a year after the trial, President George W. Bush signed the Unborn Victims of Violence Act which made it a crime to harm a preborn baby human during an assault on a pregnant woman. In other words, in the eyes of both state (California) and federal law, attacking a pregnant woman is legally the same thing as attacking two people.

The inconsistency is as obvious as it is galling. Even if Laci had survived his attack, Scott Peterson could have been sentenced to death for killing his unborn son Conner alone.

However, had Laci decided to walk into a Planned Parenthood facility in California the same day, she could have killed Conner with no legal repercussions at all.

Everyone knows this is erratic and indefensible logic. But since the culture currently embraces the "abortion is a moral choice to be made between a woman and her doctor" (Position A) mindset, politicians will not make any moves to rectify their embarrassing self-contradictions.

2. In late 2017, Republican Governor John Kasich of Ohio signed into law a statute that makes it illegal for unborn children diagnosed with Down syndrome to be targeted for abortion on that basis alone. Both Indiana and North Dakota already have similar laws on their books.

    The announcement of this legislation was a victory for Frank Stephens, a grown man who just months before was shockingly forced to justify his existence before a Congressional hearing. Born with Down syndrome, Frank has become a vocal advocate for those with the genetic disorder, telling the congressional committee that his life is "worth living" as he criticized those who believe fetuses with his condition should be aborted:

"Whatever you learn today, please remember this: I am a man with Down syndrome and my life is worth living. I completely understand that the people pushing this particular 'final solution' are saying that people like me should not exist. That view is deeply prejudiced by an outdated idea of life with Down syndrome."

Frank's concerns are sadly well-grounded. The extraordinary advances in prenatal testing and research has led to many wonderful, life-saving, life-improving techniques and treatments for babies in the womb. But as with any scientific advancements, those innovations can be used for nefarious purposes as well.

In Iceland, for example, the country now boasts a near 100% murder rate on unborn babies diagnosed with

Down syndrome in the womb. You might recall that CBS News celebrated that devastating reality with this jarring headline: "Iceland is on pace to virtually eliminate Down syndrome through abortion."[1] The story that followed was as bad as the headline, frighteningly bordering on congratulatory:

"With the rise of prenatal screening tests across Europe and the United States, the number of babies born with Down syndrome has significantly decreased, but few countries have come as close to eradicating Down syndrome births as Iceland."[2]

Missing from the report was the critical observation that precisely *nothing* has been done in Iceland about Down syndrome. All that was occurring there was that Iceland was killing everyone who had the condition. They weren't curing anything; they were killing. This is like solving the problem of poverty in the third world with nukes.

Yet as states like Ohio, Indiana, and North Dakota move to affirm the obvious reality that humans like

Frank Stephens are every bit as worthy of protection as the rest of us, a daunting and obvious inconsistency emerges.

Keep in mind it was the same Governor John Kasich who a year before (in 2016) vetoed a law that would have made it illegal for doctors to target *any* child in the womb whose heartbeat was detectable. Think Kasich's position through logically: if someone wants to kill a baby in the womb because she has Down syndrome, that is heartless, immoral, and illegal; but if someone wants to kill a baby in the womb because she is coming at an inconvenient time, that's morally acceptable.

Kasich is smart enough to know what the rest of us know – such an inconsistent stance is morally, constitutionally, and intellectually absurd. But since it is Position A, and Position A is where the votes are, Kasich will play along.

3. Finally, consider the last two Vice Presidential choices for the national

Democratic Party in America: Joe
Biden, the former Senator who
served two terms as Vice President
under Barack Obama, and Tim Kaine,
the former Virginia Governor,
Senator and Democratic National
Committee Chairman who was
Hillary Clinton's running mate in their
failed 2016 bid.

Debating Republican Vice-
Presidential nominee Paul Ryan in
2012, Joe Biden made the following
statement on national television:

*"My religion defines who I am, and I've
been a practicing Catholic my whole life.
And has particularly informed my social
doctrine. The Catholic social doctrine
talks about taking care of those who --
who can't take care of themselves, people
who need help. With regard to -- with
regard to abortion, I accept my church's
position on abortion as a -- what we call
a (inaudible) doctrine. Life begins at
conception in the church's judgment. I
accept it in my personal life. But I refuse
to impose it on equally devout Christians
and Muslims and Jews, and I just refuse
to impose that on others."*[3]

Lest there be any confusion, or anyone suggest he merely misspoke, Vice President Biden doubled down on that same position just three years later in an interview with a Jesuit-run magazine called *America*:

"I'm prepared to accept that at the moment of conception there's human life and being, but I'm not prepared to say that to other God-fearing [and] non-God-fearing people that have a different view. Abortion is always wrong. All the principles of my faith, [which] I make no excuse for attempting to live up to — I don't all the time. But I'm not prepared to impose doctrine that I'm prepared to accept on the rest of [the country]."[4]

For his part, Tim Kaine had articulated precisely the same sentiments several years earlier. Appearing on *Meet the Press* with host David Gregory to discuss the 2008 presidential campaign as DNC Chairman, Kaine's shocking performance represented yet another incredible demonstration of our society's deterioration into moral confusion. Regarding the sanctity of life, the two had this exchange:

2. Stop Waiting on Politicians

Gregory: When do you believe human rights begin?

Kaine: Well, um, human, human rights broadly, my church teaches, and I do believe that human rights begin early in life at conception or shortly thereafter. And that is my personal belief. But I do not believe the force of the criminal law should compel, uh, others to necessarily follow that to the greatest degree...but you shouldn't be talking about overturning Roe v. Wade or criminalizing women and their doctors.[5]

For anyone truly paying attention, both Biden and Kaine committed the unthinkable on national television. They both made the case that in certain circumstances, with certain victims, murder can and should be legally permissible in the United States. Notice that neither Tim Kaine nor Joe Biden contended that what is conceived in the womb is *not* a human being. Scientifically and medically untenable as it may be, that still remains the standard defense offered by most on the humanist left who seek to justify this morally outrageous act of child sacrifice. They typically suggest that the baby in the womb is nothing but a glob of tissue and cells that is not entitled to any human rights.

But not these high-ranking, high-profile leaders of the Democrat Party. Neither is saying, "I don't believe the child in the womb is a human being, and so therefore I think it is acceptable to destroy that pre-human mass of cells." No, both Kaine and Biden are admitting and *agreeing* that the being in the womb is fully human from the moment of conception.

But then, in a sort of ghastly sidestep, both men say even though they acknowledge the humanity of the child in the womb, society shouldn't be able to use the force of law to impose that view on others who may want to kill the human baby. What kind of a position is that? What kind of men are these?

This is, after all, the furthest thing from a sophisticated stance that someone could take. In fact, if any of us were to apply it consistently, think where it would lead. Imagine me saying, "Obviously I believe that you are a human being entitled to a right to live. But that's my personal belief and I don't think I can impose that belief on others. In other words, if someone else decides you *don't* have a right to live, I don't think it should be illegal for them to kill you." If this isn't the very definition of moral and intellectual bankruptcy, those terms have no meaning.

And yet, Kaine wasn't laughed out of the *Meet the Press* studio. Biden wasn't unceremoniously dumped from the Obama presidential ticket. Neither one of them were publicly reprimanded or even called upon to answer for be-clowning themselves by making an unequivocal case for legalizing murder in America.

Maybe that's because we can't think critically as a people anymore. Or maybe it's our tribal political alliances and allegiance to worn-out maxims and tired clichés. But whatever it is, it's embarrassing. Simply take Biden or Kaine's statement and substitute *any other moral issue* in the place of abortion to realize the backwards cowardice this reveals in us:

"Well, um, human, human rights broadly, my church teaches, and I do believe that human rights apply equally to all races and ethnicities. And that is my personal belief. But I do not believe the force of the criminal law should compel, uh, others to necessarily follow that to the greatest degree...but you shouldn't be talking about overturning Dred Scott or criminalizing plantation owners and slave traders."

See how intellectually and morally ridiculous that sounds? This is one reason why these issues of human rights stand out at me so vividly. As a student and teacher of U.S. history I am haunted by the fact that we have been here before.

The similarities are chilling: then – as now – a large contingent of our population believed it was acceptable that some of their fellow men were deprived of their most basic natural rights simply due to their station. They too considered themselves to be "pro-choice," maintaining that it was a constitutionally protected privilege of some to wield the taskmaster's whip over inferior countrymen.

2. Stop Waiting on Politicians

To justify the immorality, the slave-owning south relied on a tragic Supreme Court ruling in *Dred Scott v. Sanford* that declared slaves to be rightful property of their owners, not viable human beings entitled to protection under the law. As a result, countless Americans suffered brutal and inhuman treatment, even losing their lives.

Today, "position A" for our culture largely embraces and reflects the slave-owners' ideology. The choice to wield the plantation masters' whip has given way to the choice to operate the abortionists' chainsaw forceps. To justify the immorality, those who affirm this position rely on a tragically flawed Supreme Court ruling in *Roe v. Wade* that declared small humans in the womb to be the property of their mothers, not viable human beings entitled to protection under the law. As a result, millions of Americans have been, and continue to be, brutally and inhumanly dismembered.

The parallels, while astonishing, are admittedly imperfect:

1. Remember that though some slaves suffered brutal and vicious treatment, the deaths of the enslaved does not even begin to approach the number of children who have been executed through abortion.

2. While slaves were deplorably denied their inalienable right to freedom, the aborted have been denied their even more fundamental right to life.

3. While our culture eventually found the moral courage to end the dreadful practice of slavery, the monstrous evil of abortion continues largely unabated.

If our civilization is to survive, we must end the killing.

We must, as previous generations, find the strength and courage necessary to illuminate the gap between our culture's obsession with convenience and self-gratification and the eternal truths espoused in our Declaration of Independence.

We must end our people's apathy

towards evil by forcing it out of the shadows and into the daylight, and exposing the shame it brings upon our generation.

We must do our part in making this a more perfect union by demanding a society that doesn't deny, but rather celebrates an unalienable right to life for all men – convenient or not.

We must instruct the minds and once again awaken the consciences of our people to the dignity and worth of every man made in the image of God, reaffirming that uniquely American belief in the value of each individual.

We must refute the dismissive attitude of those who would relegate this topic to being a mere political problem or personal matter, and instead testify to its fundamental importance.

As I mentioned before, our society's respect for life determines its destiny; consequently no other question deserves or demands more attention, from every quarter. We must therefore passionately and relentlessly press the issue, dismantling the wicked and faulty grounds upon which this tragic ritual has been built.

We must reveal the destination of our current national path, present the culture with our better alternative and demand that this is a time for choosing.

But how can we do that? So many whose hearts and minds are convicted on this issue don't even know where to begin. My objective is that once you finish this book you won't be among their number.

3

INDEFENSIBLE LAW, GHASTLY SCIENCE

One of the major problems we have in the debate over the sanctity of life is that we are easily distracted by peripheral issues. Too often we are mired and bogged down talking about emotionally charged circumstances like abortions in the exceptional cases of rape and incest, and consequently lose sight of what should be the starting point of our discussion.

As was frighteningly revealed in Tim Kaine's interview and Joe Biden's debate, any justification for the act of abortion relies on the idea that the aborted fetus is not human. Consider:

If what is conceived in the womb is a human being, any abortion would then be tantamount to murder. Those who argue in favor of abortion rights would be put in the unenviable position of trying to make the case that though it is human, the child's residence in the womb justifies it being killed.

In other words, human rights would be subjectively dependent upon the location of the human – not exactly a sustainable rationale. This was what made Kaine and Biden's defense so appalling. They both acknowledged the humanity of the child in the womb, but then said they thought it should remain legal to brutally murder the child. This grotesque position is totally untenable – something that even the fiercest defenders of abortion recognize.

If you doubt that, go back to the landmark *Roe v. Wade* case in 1973. During oral arguments, Justice Potter Stewart asked Sarah Weddington, the attorney representing the abortion lobby:

> *"If it were established that an unborn fetus is a person, you would have an almost*

impossible case here, would you not?"

Weddington audibly laughed as she was forced to acknowledge:

"I would have a very difficult case."

Justice Stewart pushed further by asking the obvious:

> *"This would be the equivalent to after the child was born...if the mother thought it bothered her health having the child around, she could have it killed. Isn't that correct?"*

Weddington sheepishly granted:

"That's correct."[6]

Remember Weddington was as committed to the cause of legal abortion as anyone. But her commitment was clearly predicated upon the (now disproven) idea that the unborn child was merely a clump of cells that lacked humanity. Even those who won the so-called "right to abortion" acknowledged in the course of the proceedings that if the humanity of the unborn was ever established, abortion would be homicide on par with executing an infant or toddler.

This shocking and eye-opening exchange is what prompted the author of the *Roe* ruling, Justice Harry Blackmun himself, to acknowledge that the humanity of the fetus is the crux of the debate. In his majority opinion, Blackmun wrote,

> *"If this suggestion of personhood is established, the appellant's case [for abortion rights], of course, collapses."*[7]

Again, Blackmun understood that if the Court legally recognized that the unborn child was a human person, they could never give tacit approval for abortion without undermining every law prohibiting murder in the United States.

So why do we have legal abortion? Because amazingly, after noting the supreme significance of the question of humanity, Blackmun's majority decided,

> *"We need not resolve the difficult question of when life begins."*[8]

What? This inexplicable inconsistency begins to demonstrate why the *Roe* decision is commonly regarded as one of the most vulnerable in the history of the United States Supreme Court, and why after nearly a half century of precedent it remains ripe for repeal.

Even abortion defenders like Laurence Tribe of Harvard Law School acknowledge that,

> *"One of the most curious things about Roe is that, behind its own verbal smokescreen, the substantive judgment on which it rests is nowhere to be found."*[9]

What's more, Justice Blackmun's own law clerk, author Edward Lazarus, penned this stinging indictment of the incoherency of the *Roe* decision:

> *"As a matter of constitutional interpretation and judicial method, Roe borders on the indefensible. I say this as someone utterly committed to the right to choose...and as someone who loved Roe's author like a grandfather...A constitutional right to privacy broad enough to include abortion has no*

> *meaningful foundation in*
> *constitutional text, history, or*
> *precedent. "[10]*

Even more damaging to its legitimacy, the case for abortion rights has no basis in medical science. After hearing the testimony of some of the world's most well-respected doctors, physicians, and medical scientists on the issue of life in the womb, a Senate Subcommittee Report in 1981 concluded,

> *"Physicians, biologists, and other*
> *scientists agree that conception*
> *marks the beginning of the life of a*
> *human being - a being that is*
> *alive and is a member of the*
> *human species. There is*
> *overwhelming agreement on this*
> *point in countless medical,*
> *biological, and scientific*
> *writings...no witness raised any*
> *evidence to refute the biological*
> *fact that from the moment of*
> *conception there exists a distinct*
> *individual being who is alive and*
> *is of the human species. "[11]*

"No witness." "Biological fact." Think

about that. A literal Who's Who of medical and biological sciences testified – and this was almost four decades ago without all our current understanding about human development. Yet even then Dr. Jerome LeJune of the University of Descartes confirmed that:

> *"After fertilization has taken place a new human being has come into being. [It] is no longer a matter of taste or opinion...it is plain experimental evidence."*[12]

Professor Micheline Matthews-Roth's testified that:

> *"It is incorrect to say that biological data cannot be decisive...It is scientifically correct to say that an individual human life begins at conception."*[13]

Not one of these expert medical minds – regardless of their personal opinions on the issue of abortion – would deny the obvious truth that what is conceived in the womb is fully living, and fully human.

And that reality is where we must start. It's where all conversations regarding abortion and the sanctity of life must begin.

Those who advocate for life-destroying practices must be aggressively exposed as standing against all scientific, medical, logical and rational thought.

And the opportunities to do this are voluminous if we pay attention.

Consider what happened at Fort Lewis College in Durango, Colorado, just weeks before the 2010 midterm elections. Debating the two sides of Colorado Amendment 62 (an amendment that would have defined the child in the womb as a person and therefore entitled to legal protection) were spokesmen for Personhood USA and an organization called Advocates for Choice, a college outreach group affiliated with the country's largest abortion mill, Planned Parenthood.

After being presented with the biological evidence of the unborn child's humanity, a spokeswoman for the Advocates for Choice proudly proclaimed to the audience:

> *"We are not going to try to use science or evidence, the fact of the matter is, this is,*

this is opinion. We all have our own opinions as far as when human life begins."[14]

The utter senselessness inherent in such a statement is hard to digest. Is it seriously the position of Planned Parenthood and their allies that what constitutes human life and what does not is merely a matter of personal opinion? A murderer is no longer a murderer if he or she simply declares that he doesn't believe in the humanity of his victim?

This relativistic tripe makes a mockery of what is legitimately and scientifically known: that the terms "embryo" and "fetus" – just as other terms like "infant" or "adult" – don't refer to nonhumans. They refer to humans at particular stages of development. But this blatant antipathy towards science, expressed by the Advocates for Choice, was just beginning.

Later in the debate, that same Planned Parenthood spokeswoman enlightened the audience that:

"What is inside a body that cannot function

outside its host is not a child."[15]

Leaving aside the scarring use of the word "host" to define the precious relationship between a mother and her baby, this argument represents a transparent strategy of misdirection. Viability – that is, the ability to function independently and autonomously – is an arbitrary line that is drawn to determine what a person can do. It does not determine what a person is. Highlighting that significant detail literally implodes this entire line of faulty logic.

Yet seemingly undeterred by the fact that they had openly declared themselves to be enemies of science, those Planned Parenthood affiliates continued:

> *"We're talking about science as if it is something that is absolutely concrete, like there is absolute proof that there is life and there is not life.*"[16]

Knowing how to respond to that kind of a statement can be difficult, because it demonstrates not only a total disregard of simple biology, but a bizarre contempt for rational thinking. Ignorance is frustrating. But taking pride in ignorance is scary.

And how can we not be frightened when after hearing these legal abortion advocates continue leveling bizarre statements in this debate like "science cannot be applied to my body," and "the heart doesn't beat 'til 24 weeks,"[17] we pause to consider that through their legislative surrogates, these are the very people who have crafted our national policy on abortion? Medical science has established the heart begins beating at just 3 weeks, over 5 months earlier than the abortion crowd alleged while attempting to justify their position.

Far from any devotion to the sanctity of science or the Constitution, our humanist culture perpetuates what has become a macabre yet sickeningly profitable ritual of infant-killing by trampling rationality, appealing instead to the shifting sands of moral relativism.

4

ALWAYS ASK THIS QUESTION

Nowhere is that moral relativism more apparent than in the infamous 1992 Supreme Court case that upheld legal abortion in America, *Planned Parenthood v. Casey*.

Finally given an opportunity to provide some clarity to the muddled mess the *Roe v. Wade* decision had left in its wake, five justices of the Supreme Court attempted to articulate a more precise justification for the legality and morality of human fetus killing. Their pitiful effort shows that even when given almost 20 years to come up with a better explanation for the gruesome practice, the brightest legal minds can't offer anything beyond a self-defeating quagmire of personal preferences.

They wrote:

> *"Some of us as individuals find abortion offensive to our most basic principles of morality, but that cannot control our decision. Our obligation is to define the liberty of all, not to mandate our own moral code. At the heart of liberty is the right to define one's own concept of existence, of meaning, of the universe, and of the mystery of human life."*[25]

Attempting to fully grasp the breathtaking ignorance of this proclamation is a daunting task. What is the purpose of any law (or any court, for that matter) if it is not to maintain or preserve morality? That's what laws and court opinions do: declare something to be right and something to be wrong.

Again, imagine consistently applying the Court's *Planned Parenthood v. Casey* logic by saying to the slave,

"We find slavery offensive to our most basic principles of morality, but that cannot control our decision."

Or perhaps,

"We find child molesting offensive to our most basic principles of morality, but that cannot control our decision."

Such foolishness is to be expected of juvenile minds, but it is inexcusable coming from those who have in many ways become our black-robed oligarchs.

Moreover, in what amounts to a mammoth definition of liberty, the Supreme Court basically endorses societal anarchy by proclaiming that any concept of right or wrong is left up to the individual. This is the bumper sticker mentality: "Don't like abortion? Don't have one."

While this may satisfy the intellectual curiosity of those whose consciences have been seared by humanism and the prideful arrogance it inevitably breeds, it should terrify us that the highest court in the land has been reduced to such foolishness.

4. Always Ask This Question

Rather than diligent allegiance to the authority of Moral Law, they have deferred to the wisdom of what they read on the back window of the minivan while parked at a stoplight. As before, simply apply any other moral issue to this ruling's pseudo-wisdom and you see the problem: "Don't like slavery? Don't own one." "Don't like theft? Don't steal."

This is the consequence of having a predetermined end that you know violates Moral Law, and yet trying to find any way to justify it. It's why Judge Robert Bork fittingly excoriated the five justices who signed their names to this insanity by writing:

> *"One would think that grown men and women, purporting to practice an intellectual profession, would themselves choose to die with dignity, right in the courtroom, before writing sentences like those."*[26]

It's also why columnist and professor Jeffrey Rosen, the legal affairs editor for the liberal *The New Republic* magazine wrote a decade after the *Casey* ruling in 2003:

"Thirty years after Roe, the finest constitutional minds in the country still have not been able to produce a constitutional justification...that is substantially more convincing than Justice Harry Blackmun's famously artless opinion itself. As a result, the pro-choice majority asks nominees to swear allegiance to the decision without being able to identify an intelligible principle to support it."[27]

That inability to tie this gruesome practice of child sacrifice to any logical justification compels those who continue supporting it to willfully assume the role of fools. Only by feigning complete obliviousness to the most basic questions can they escape the inexcusable cowardice that defines their refusal to defend the rights of inconvenient children.

Consider as an example of this weakness the asinine response U.S. President Barack Obama gave to minister Rick Warren during the 2008 presidential campaign. At the Saddleback Civil Forum on the Presidency, Obama and Warren had the following exchange:

> Warren: "Now, let's deal with abortion; 40 million abortions since Roe v. Wade. As a pastor, I have to deal with this all of the time, all of the pain and all of the conflicts. I know this is a very complex issue. Forty million abortions, at what point does a baby get human rights, in your view?"

> Obama: "Well, you know, I think that whether you're looking at it from a theological perspective or a scientific perspective, answering that question with specificity, you know, is above my pay grade."[28]

Simply put, questions that define our respect for human rights cannot be above anyone's pay grade, particularly our leaders. Obama's frustrating response shows the dramatic paucity of leadership we are now experiencing. How far we have come from the days of Abraham Lincoln. He too faced a great moral question, and yet he refused to equivocate, for better or for worse. Choosing to stand for right rather than compromise with wickedness, he threw down the gauntlet by declaring:

> *"A house divided against itself cannot stand. I believe this government cannot endure permanently half slave and half free. I do not expect the Union to be dissolved; I do not expect the house to fall; but I do expect that it will cease to be divided. It will become all one thing, or all the other. Either the opponents of slavery will arrest the further spread of it, and place it where the public mind shall rest in the belief that it is in the course of ultimate extinction; or its advocates will push it forward till it shall become alike lawful in all the States, old as well as new, North as well as South."*[29]

Had Lincoln deflected the issue of slavery by suggesting it was "above his pay grade," he surely would not hold such an esteemed place of reverence in the collective hearts of his countrymen. Likely, he would be regarded for what he would have been: a coward.

Further, consider the disappointing irony that without Lincoln's fortitude and moral courage, it is highly unlikely a man with the racial and ethnic identity of Barack Obama would have ever taken the presidential oath of office. Yet when given the opportunity to walk in the heroic footsteps of the Great Emancipator, Obama took a pass.

Despite his pretending, Barack Obama is not an ignorant man; he knows the answer to Rick Warren's question. But Obama is also smart enough to recognize that he can't do what his Vice President (Biden) and his party chairman (Kaine).

He knows he can't acknowledge his awareness that a child in the womb is fully human and should be entitled to human rights. Because having never in the history of his legislative or executive career supported a measure to protect those rights, he is cognizant of the ethical fallout that would follow such an admission.

Consequently, he merely answered Rick Warren that way as part of a tactical strategy to avoid answering questions that would expose his fidelity to "Position A" despite knowing it to be intellectually unjustified and morally indefensible.

Of course, he's far from alone. Having thoroughly lost the abortion debate on every ground upon which it is fought – constitutional, legal, ethical, moral, logical – the popular trend within the movement for legalized child killing is to follow President Obama's hollow yet effective approach and merely play dumb.

But this last resort reveals the Achilles Heel of the abortion lobby. In every abortion conversation Christians must commit ourselves to not moving an inch in the discussion until this fundamental question is answered: what is in the womb?

By acting confused and pleading ignorance to that simple question, secularists commit themselves to an unsustainable war of attrition. Eventually, they will be exposed.

That's exactly what occurred in Colorado back in December of 2008. Appearing on radio host Bob Enyart's program, *Bob Enyart Live*, abortion advocate Ilana Goldman was stumped by questions most 2nd graders could answer with ease. That isn't a pejorative insult of Ms. Goldman. It's a serious assessment – I have a 2nd grader and she had no problem answering these questions.

Her embarrassing performance on Enyart's show should leave no one with the mistaken impression that Ms. Goldman, the president of Women's Campaign Forum and heralded as one of Washington's "Eight Women to Watch," is ignorant. What was revealed was what eventually happens to those who commit themselves to defending the indefensible.

Like Obama, Goldman quickly realized that even simple statements of commonly accepted biological fact would dismantle her entirely unethical position, so she attempted to avoid making them. She took an "above my pay grade" approach; but unlike Rick Warren, Bob Enyart didn't let her off the hook:

Enyart: "You just said that, 'We believe that life begins after birth.' I'm sure that's not the case, right? You know that the baby in the womb when he's sucking his thumb, playing with his toes, if they're twins they grab one another, the baby learns his mother's voice as compared to the voice of a nurse or doctor; the baby can actually learn melodies to songs. And let me ask you, is it living? I mean, personhood is one issue, and being alive – like a plant is alive and a rabbit is alive, but a plant is not a person – so whether you're alive, that's a separate matter from whether something's a person. So do you agree that it's alive?"

Goldman: (quiet pause)

Enyart: "Just in the biological sense: is it living or is it dead?"

Goldman: "I'm gonna be perfectly honest, I, uh, I, what you're saying does not make sense to me - "

Enyart: "I'm asking you if it's living."

4. Always Ask This Question

Goldman: "If you, if you want to talk about what is happ –, what are, what are the realities – "

Enyart: "I realize you don't want to address the issue of what it is. You'd rather skip over that to talk about strong emotions and majority opinions – "

Goldman: "I'm not, I'm not skipping over that. I'm really answering your question."

Enyart: "Okay, well then could you answer this question? Could you answer this – because you said life begins after birth, I think you overstated your own case – but is it living? Is it living or is it dead? I mean some th –, there's inanimate things like rocks are not living. So the fetus in the womb, it's sucking its thumb, playing with its toes, sleeping, it dreams, is it living? I'm not saying is it a person. Is it living?"

Goldman: (quiet pause) "I am unwilling to engage – "

Enyart: "You're afraid of that question."

Goldman: "No, I'm not afraid of that question."

Enyart: "Well then answer it! Is it living?

It's either living or dead."

Goldman: "I think, I think, uh, I think the definition of life – what is life, when does life begin, these are questions that people reasonably struggle with."

...

Enyart: "Is it alive?"

Goldman: "I – I want to be perfectly clear."

Enyart: "Yeah."

Goldman: "I am not afraid of this question. I just think that it's a ridiculous question."

...

Enyart: "Okay, before I know what I can do with it, I have to know what it is. Can I dispose of it? Can I throw it out? Can I kill it? Well the question is 'what is it.' And that seems to be – Ilana even though you're a leader on this issue, you seem to be afraid to address that. Let me ask you this: what is a fetus? What is a fetus?"

Goldman: (long uncomfortable pause) "What – what's your game here? I, I'm not going to get into larger questions of, of, of -"

4. Always Ask This Question

Enyart: "Of the baby."[30]

When I play the audio of that debate at speaking engagements, the audience is usually laughing, sometimes hysterically, by the end. Though that's understandable given the incredibly simple questions this bright woman pretended to not understand, when you realize that over a million American children die every year because our laws are held hostage by such anti-intellectualism, our laughter should turn to despair.

This barbaric ritual of abortion has been in existence for over four decades. In our enlightened and sophisticated era, we have allowed a draconian practice that mirrors – only with more refined tools – the animalistic child sacrifice of ancient times. They sacrificed their children to Molech on the pagan altars; we sacrifice ours to the god of selfishness on the altar of convenience.

Such an acknowledgement is not merely an indictment of those who tenaciously pursue the expansion of this kind of wickedness, but also those who claim to oppose it while refusing to stop it.

Now is a time for choosing. Either what is conceived in the womb is not a human person, or it is. If it's not, then logically there should be no moral or ethical limits placed upon the practice of abortion. If it is not a human being, it is not worthy of protection or of human rights, and there is no excuse to infringe upon the autonomy of any woman.

But if it is a human being, the very words of our Constitution and Declaration of Independence, the fundamental principles of Western Civilization, and the entire weight of divine Moral Law that supersedes every law of man, converge to demand we safeguard the life, liberty, and well-being of all human persons, particularly the most vulnerable.

This is not, and has never been a question of Republican/Democrat, conservative/liberal, or right/left. It is a question of submission to God's Moral Law.

If it is a human being, we have no choice but to speak forcefully and without hesitation against the evil being done in the false name of choice. We must paraphrase the words of our forebears like abolitionist William Lloyd Garrison:

> *"I am a believer in that portion of the Declaration of American Independence in which it is set forth, as among self-evident truths, 'that all men are created equal; that they are endowed by their Creator with certain inalienable rights; that among these are life, liberty, and the pursuit of happiness.' Hence, I am pro-life. Hence, I cannot but regard oppression in every form – and most of all, that which turns a man into a thing – with indignation and abhorrence. Convince me that one man may rightfully take the life of another, and I will no longer subscribe to the Declaration of Independence. Convince me that life is not the inalienable birthright of every human being, of whatever complexion or clime, and I will give that instrument to the consuming fire...Numerically, the contest may be an unequal one, for the time being; but the Author of liberty and the Source of justice, the adorable God, is more than multitudinous, and he will defend the right. My crime is that I will not go with the multitude to do evil. My singularity is that*

when I say that freedom is of God and abortion is of the devil, I mean just what I say. My fanaticism is that I insist on the American people abolishing abortion or ceasing to prate of the rights of man... [31]

If it is a human being, there can be no compromises made by which we allow them to be denied human rights and be destroyed.

If it is a human being we recognize that there is never a situation where the life of the mother requires intentionally killing the living human child inside her. In the extraordinarily rare cases where a mother's life might be endangered by carrying the child to term, a sane and moral society would obviously allow the baby to remain in the sanctuary of the womb as long as possible before removing him in order to save the life of the mother. And then every known medical effort must be made to save the life of the child. Save them both. There is no logical alternative.

If it is a human being, abortion is never justified, and those who argue for it – who argue for legalized homicide (specifically, in this case, feticide) – must be intellectually shamed and morally rebuked.

It is unquestionable that respect for human life is the grand moral dilemma of our time. Abortion may be the current manifestation of the larger issue, yet the science, constitutionality, morality, and ethics of it were decided long ago. All that remains is for us to have the moral courage to act upon self-evident truth.

Christ followers must again find themselves at the forefront of this paramount struggle for full human rights, desirous of making ours the generation that posterity looks on with fondness as the one that put an end to the American holocaust...the one that finally turned the page on this most embarrassing and repugnant chapter of our history.

But what part do you and I play?

Understanding the epic failure and tragic capitulation of our political class is one thing; proactively leading corrective action is something entirely different. And that, far more than lacking the wisdom, righteousness, or motivation, is where we so often struggle.

Again, it's not failing to know what is right, it's failing to know what to do to make things right that has come to define our pro-life movement in America.

And the reason may just have everything to do with an identity crisis.

5

YOU AREN'T A POLITICIAN

You aren't a politician. At least not in the traditional sense. According to statistics from Pew, only 2% of the American population say they have ever run for public office.[25] That's not very many of you.

But keep in mind that the 2% number cited by Pew includes every public office in the country, including positions like Dog Catcher, Town Council, Township Trustee, or School Board. Now, I don't make that stipulation to slight or diminish the importance of any of those roles, or the sacrifice it takes to be a public servant of any kind. I'm simply pointing out that almost all of those 2% are people serving in positions that have little to no impact on abortion law in the United States.

Yet whenever the topics of abortion, infanticide, euthanasia, or suicide come up – either in churches, seminars, rallies, or banquets – it is almost always addressed in strictly political terms:

- It's addressed from the depressing perspective of statistics – the millions of children who have been lost due to our cultural self-worship.

- It's addressed from the infuriating perspective of an out-of-control judiciary – black-robed lawyers imposing their unelected will on the masses through judicial review.

- It's addressed from the strategic perspective of legislation – what regulations have slowed the abortion or suicide rates most effectively, and what laws have been most helpful in closing the doors of abortion mills.

And thousands upon thousands of people who have no control over the statistics, no power to affect the judiciary, no ability to craft legislation sit, listen, cry, applaud, write checks, and walk out the door broken hearted and even angry until something happens later that day to distract them.

How do I know that is what occurs all the time? Because for years as a prolific speaker at many of these events and venues, it is precisely how I addressed these topics. I hammered away at the ignorance of our laws and hypocrisy of our lawmakers, and received more standing ovations for my words than I can recall. But to be brutally honest, I'm not sure how much any of those talks ever helped anyone or furthered the cause.

Please don't misunderstand. God is sovereign, and that means He is over and authoritative in every area of human life, including politics. God's truth needs to be spoken and heeded in the White House every bit as much as it does in the church house. What I'm saying is that in all of my pro-life speaking engagements, accounting for tens of thousands of people, I can probably count on two hands the number of individuals who heard my speeches and actually had even the slightest possibility of speaking the truth I shared into the ears of a president or Supreme Court justice.

All this hit me like a ton of bricks in January of 2017 when I was invited to speak at the March for Life event in Fort Wayne, Indiana. The organizer, a wonderful woman named Cathie Humbarger, had asked me to come and share a positive, uplifting message that inspired people and motivated them with what they could do in this fight for life. I'm sure with all the years that Cathie has been in the business of advocating for human rights she has heard on more than one occasion, "It was a great event, but what can I *do*?"

To be honest, I prepared what was a fairly standard, fiery pro-life message that centered on the political side of this cause. It's what I always did, and I felt like it always went well. When I arrived at the venue early I was looking over my notes as Cathie approached with newly elected Congressman Jim Banks – a man I had met years before at a different speaking engagement, and whose political rise had been meteoric since that time. After catching up briefly with Jim, Cathie gave me a list of the other political dignitaries that would be there.

I sat back down as the auditorium began to fill up and I looked at that list. Ten names. I turned around and looked at the auditorium that would soon be at capacity, estimating about 2,000 seats. It hit me right then that my political speech that focused on courts, Congress, laws, and rights would leave 1,990 people (99.5% of my audience) wondering what they should do.

All over my body I felt that sinking sensation that you get when you're in school and the teacher starts to collect the assignment that you completely forgot about the night before. I borrowed a pen from the person next to me, pulled the front page of my speech manuscript from its plastic covering in my binder, turned it over and began to scribble new thoughts.

I don't think I've told Cathie this (and what are the odds she'll ever read this book?) but with all the time and effort she put into that event, I wrote the keynote speech in ten minutes, finishing it up right when I sat down following the Pledge of Allegiance.

When I was introduced, the emcee mentioned how we were gathering that day at a "defining moment" in the life of our country. The inauguration of Donald Trump had happened the day before and there was great excitement at the prospect of leaving behind the disastrous (for the right-to-life cause) Obama years, and great anticipation of how Trump's presidency might reshape the nation's courts. It was the perfect lead-in for me.

I walked to the stage, led off with a short anecdote and then said the following:

> *"If I might be so bold, what happens in Washington is not your defining moment. You don't write the laws or vote on them.*
>
> *You don't develop alliances, pigeonhole legislation, or deal with lobbyists. The fate of the tragic abortion laws that govern our nation today is not resting on your*

shoulders."

Then, walking over to stand right in front of Congressman Banks I said,

"What happens in Washington, D.C. is not your burden to bear, friends. It's his.

God has brought Representative Banks to the palace, just like the ancient Queen Esther, for such a time as this. To take up the cause of the innocent, to defend children, and to refuse to compromise when the cost is even one life.

And God will judge him according to how he does those very things. That is a tremendous burden to carry, and I beg you not to let a day go by that you don't pray for Representative Banks.

The pressure to compromise and capitulate on truth is great in the halls of sophisticated men. Pray for Jim. Pray he would always remember that what moves him and motivates him should never be the fear of answering to any party, any Speaker, any President, or any voter for his actions.

He answers to the God of the Universe who is not ambivalent or confused or compromising on His stance on the question

of the value of human life.

Pray that Jim Banks never forgets that truth. Not for us or our cause. But for him.

That's his defining moment. But I'm not here to lecture or motivate Representative Banks...even though I just did one whale of a job of it, didn't I?

Banks laughed, the audience laughed, and the tension was broken. But it was one of the most important moments in any pro-life speech I've ever given, and here's why. Jesus turned the world on its head with just a handful of outcasts and unexceptional men who were committed and obedient to do what He called them to do, when and where He called them to do it.

Yet we have literally millions of people committed to the pro-life cause in this country, and we aren't able to move the needle. Why? I firmly believe the answer is because we are not fighting the battles we've been given to fight.

We're trying desperately to leave our arena and fight in an area we haven't been called, where no one is listening to us, no one cares what we think, and where we are wasting our talents. Imagine Peter, Andrew, James and John, imagine Paul and Barnabas, Timothy and Luke ignoring their calls to evangelize in their spheres of influence, instead spending their talents and efforts trying to get the attention of Roman Senators.

The phrase "bloom where you're planted" has special application here. I spent years speaking to plants, instructing them on how they could bloom in the halls of the Supreme Court, the West Wing, or the Capitol rotunda – places they will never be. And until that late morning in Fort Wayne, Indiana, I had never told any of them how they could be obedient and faithful to God in their witness and testimony for life right where He had so wisely placed them – in their schools, factories, homes, families, doctor's offices, teachers' lounges, grocery stores, church services, pubs, and hangouts.

It all changed for me that day in Fort Wayne. I hope it's about to change for you.

6

YOU'RE A BISHOP, ROOK, KNIGHT, OR PAWN

God is the Master chess player. He puts His pieces – whether we are rooks, knights, bishops, queens, or yes even pawns – exactly where they need to be, at exactly the time they need to be there in order to bring about victory. Not victory in an earthly sense – victory in an eternal sense.

And that's the first correction we need to make as witnesses to the truth about the value of human life. God hasn't called me or positioned me to change the hearts of Congress. I've not been placed in the palace like Esther, in the parliament like William Wilberforce (the man who single handedly turned the government of Britain against the slave trade), or in Congress like Jim Banks.

I've been placed in a classroom where every year I have about 100 different students I get to know closely. Can God use that in this civilizational battle for the value of life? Does He need His servants to be working diligently there every bit as much as in the Senate? Of course.

But how often do we think that way as pro-life people? We don't. We measure success on whether or not a really bad law gets changed; something which again, 99% of us have no control over whatsoever. That isn't smart, savvy, or shrewd. It's ham-fisted and ineffective.

What's a smarter way for me to measure success in my testimony for the value of human life in our culture? Let me answer that with a question: do you think it is more important that my students know I want *Roe v. Wade* overturned, or that I love and value each of them, think human life is the most sacred thing in the world – including theirs, and would be there for them with compassion if they ever had a personal crisis arise in their lives that scared them to death...say, like an unplanned pregnancy?

Have I made an impact for a Godly culture of life if my students know that I think Planned Parenthood is evil, or if they know that I love them unconditionally and would adopt their unplanned baby as my own if they needed me to? Again, don't misunderstand. It doesn't have to be either/or. I don't shy away from sharing my views publicly about how monstrous I believe abortion is, or how corrupt and vile I think the Planned Parenthood corporation has demonstrated itself to be.

But I have come to realize that my contribution to this cause *has* to be something far more than a political position for me to be obedient to God. And the same goes for you.

Is it more important that the person next to you in the factory line knows you contribute to your local Right-to-Life PAC, or that they know *why* you think God is amazing how He has a plan and special purpose for every single human life that is ever conceived?

Is it more important that your church organizes a group to harass congressmen with phone calls, or that it offers counseling for post-abortive women, supplies volunteers to local crisis pregnancy centers, and teaches the righteousness of valuing every human life unapologetically?

Let me stress again, only because I'm paranoid that I'm not articulating this clearly: Christians should *never* shy away from the truth that what is conceived in the womb is a living human being that bears the image of God. We should *never* be willing to compromise our conviction that every image bearer of God possesses an inherent worth that is inviolable. And we should *never* stop speaking that truth outwardly and openly.

But when asking what we can do to change things, we have to do more than just deal with the issue politically.

We must deal with it culturally, because

that's where God has so wisely placed us.

Kings and queens will be judged by God for their faithfulness and obedience within the palace. We pawns will be judged for our faithfulness outside the castle walls.

7

THE ROOT OF OUR PROBLEM IS SELF-WORSHIP

One of the statements I made in my Fort Wayne March for Life speech that day was this:

> *"Let those in Washington do what they will. But may we be engaging the battle every day not over our laws but over our culture. Trust that we have empowered men like Jim Banks to battle for our laws. And let Jim know that he can trust us to battle for the heart of our society."*

Everyone with a brain knows the corruption and immorality rampant in our nation's capital. But we seem to forget that D.C. is merely a reflection of our people.

Votes still decide elections, and we get the leaders we deserve. If we want to change the face of Washington, we have to first change the face of our culture and what it values.

And what does it value above everything else? What is the beginning and ending point for all our corporate and individual actions and beliefs? Me. We are a society consumed with self-interest. And it only stands to reason that a culture awash in selfishness, self-centeredness, and self-worship will see the value of "other life" degraded and denied if it stands in the way of our personal sense of gratification, autonomy, and empowerment.

Not long ago the pro-abortion Guttmacher Institute released a study entitled, "Reasons U.S. Women Have Abortions: Quantitative and Qualitative Perspectives." The study was based on a survey of thousands of women who had recently committed abortion, where they were asked to name the, "most important reason for having the abortion." The top answer given was that the "timing was wrong." Second place answer? They "couldn't afford a baby now."[26]

Though this would seem to demonstrate with certainty that the decision to exterminate your offspring is motivated primarily by self-centeredness, one such post-abortive woman named "Libby Anne" wrote on the feminist pages of online commentary site Patheos why abortion is actually quite "selfless." Yes, I'm serious. Here's what she argued:

> *"Today I don't want a dozen or more children. I don't even want eight children, or five. I don't want to be a stay at home mom. I don't want to spend ten full years pregnant or twenty years changing diapers. I don't actually particularly enjoy being pregnant. I want to work, to continue on a career that I find intellectually stimulating and fulfilling. I want to raise only a few children, but to invest in each one and raise them well. I want to choose when and if I become pregnant, to be able to have my economics and work*

situation in order, to be as prepared as possible for each child I decide to bring into this world. I have become one of those selfish, selfish women.

Except that I don't feel selfish. I feel responsible. I feel loving. I feel happy.

The truth is, not wanting a large family isn't 'selfish.' Not wanting children at all isn't 'selfish.' Wanting to plan when and how many children to have is not 'selfish.' Wanting to work outside the home isn't 'selfish.' Feeling your heart sink when you learn that you are unexpectedly and inconveniently pregnant is not 'selfish.' In fact, it's kind of normal.

You know what strikes me as selfish? Thinking your own choices are the only acceptable ones and wanting to impose those choices on everyone else. Telling other people how they should live. Expecting every woman to fit a one-size-fits-all mold you've fashioned from your reading of your holy book.

Many women have abortions not because they are 'selfish' but because they are responsible. Sixty percent of women who have abortions already have children. For some women, an abortion is the only financially acceptable option. For some women, an abortion is needed so that they can properly care for the children they already have. For some women, an abortion allows them to finish their education so that they can someday give their future children better lives than they themselves had. Women don't have abortions lightly or on a whim. "[27]

And just in case you were preparing to jump in and argue that for those women who feel they can't afford or don't want a child at the time of their pregnancy, adoption is a far better alternative to dismembering your baby, Libby disagrees:

"It's often stated that women faced

with unplanned pregnancies should just go through the pregnancy and then give the child up for adoption. This is the 'selfless' thing to do, and those who choose to abort rather than offer their child for adoption are 'selfish.' There are several problems with this argument.

First, not everyone is comfortable with the idea of having a child and letting someone else raise it, probably without ever seeing it again or knowing if it is having a good life. I know I'm not comfortable with that idea.

Second, pregnancy is an extremely difficult and arduous and invasive and inconvenient process. Pregnancy means losing control of your body for nine months, facing debilitating nausea and food aversions, a lowered immune system, a swollen belly and altered sense of gravity, physical discomfort and potential back problems, and finally, the painful and difficult process of

> *labor, followed by a recovery that takes months. Oh, and did I mention that pregnancy includes having to buy a whole new wardrobe and answer questions from family, friends, and ever-friendly strangers?"*[28]

So, let's just pause and make sure we're all following this popular explanation of how abortion is not a selfish choice. Libby has outlined her reasons to get an abortion as follows:

- She wants a small family.

- She wants to work out of the home.

- She wants to not feel uncomfortable.

- She wants to avoid nausea.

- She wants to avoid food aversion for a few months.

- She wants to avoid a weaker immune system.

- She wants to avoid a swollen belly.

- She wants to avoid an altered sense of gravity.

- She wants to avoid potential chronic back problems.

- She wants to avoid painful delivery.

- She wants to avoid long recovery.

- She wants to save money by not buying new clothes.

- She wants to avoid questions from others.

That would be 13 reasons which all, in case you missed it, begin with the phrase, "She wants." Despite her protestations to the contrary, this is the textbook definition of selfishness. Regardless of that painfully obvious fact that seems to elude her, she concludes,

> *"Abortion isn't about 'selfish' women flouting 'God's plan' for their lives. Abortion is about women in tight situations trying to make the best decisions for themselves, their current and*

*future children, and their families.
Sometimes, there are no easy
answers."[29]*

This is the blinding effect that self-interest can have on us as humans. To explain how the decision to abort is not self-interested, Libby actually says that those who choose abortion are, "trying to make the best decisions for themselves." That's literally what self-interest means. To be fair, Libby is just one of many making these bewildering and backwards arguments. The perilously feminist Ms. Magazine recently defended abortion in the same way, stating,

*"The decision to have an abortion
is rarely simple. Most women are
very cognizant of the demands of
parenthood and want to have a
family only when the time is right.
They are concerned about their
ability to provide a stable
environment for themselves and
their children."[30]*

No matter where you stand on the issue of abortion, surely any fair observer can identify the glaring self-interest that is motivating this argument. After all, procreation is the natural consequence to sexual intercourse. When a woman becomes pregnant after sex it can never be taken as abnormal or unexpected. In fact, it's precisely what should be expected.

It's a poor analogy perhaps, but the natural result of slamming my hand in a car door is broken fingers. It might not always happen, but I could hardly suggest that a broken finger was an abnormal or unexpected result of the decision to smash them in the door of my Jeep. Therefore, if someone is wanting to, "have a family only when the time is right," the obvious precaution you would take is to refrain from sexual conduct. But notice that apparently isn't even a conceivable option to the scholars at Ms. Magazine. And why not? Because it stands in the way of personal pleasure. It conflicts with the desires of *me*.

Other more honest abortion advocates will recognize the obvious self-interest behind killing children in the womb. But they justify it by saying that not all selfish acts are immoral. Ray Girn argues this point in an issue of *The Undercurrent*:

> *"When a student studies hard to get into graduate school, he is not immoral. When a young couple saves money for years to buy their dream house, they are not immoral. When America's Founders rebelled again the British and enshrined the 'Pursuit of Happiness' as a political ideal, they were not immoral. All of these were self-interested actions, yet they are clearly moral. These individuals are pursuing long-term goals on principle, neither sacrificing themselves to others, nor sacrificing others to themselves. Nothing could be more moral than that.*
>
> *When a woman goes against her entire culture and gets an abortion-because she doesn't want a child at this point in her life-her actions are similarly moral. She is choosing to value her own life, rather than to give in to familial or societal pressures to*

sacrifice her life because of scriptural dogma and raise a child she is not motivated to raise. "[31]

If you injured your brain trying to complete all the mental contortions necessary to make sense out of those paragraphs you aren't alone. There are so many false parallels and incoherent premises articulated in those few words it is difficult to even know how to unpack it. First, each of the examples the author gives could actually be regarded as selfless, not selfish. The young couple is sacrificing momentary personal pleasures for a long term objective that will benefit more than just themselves. America's Founders risked (and some lost) everything in order to provide a better way of life for their posterity. Surely no one with a functioning brain could actually analogize such self-sacrifice with the act of killing your posterity so that you can enjoy immediate personal pleasure, right?

What Girn is really attempting here is to redefine the entire concept of morality:

"Defenders of abortion need to

7. The Root of Our Problem is Self-Worship

> *challenge the Religious Right at its*
> *root. They need to challenge the*
> *morality of sacrifice. They need to*
> *embrace the fact that abortion is*
> *the selfish choice, and then*
> *explain that that's precisely why it*
> *is the moral choice.*"[32]

Did you catch that? The "morality of sacrifice" needs to be challenged. Abortion is the moral choice not in spite of, but *because* it is the selfish choice.

This is where our "me"-obsessed culture is leading us. We celebrate sexual decadence because it gratifies our base urges. We freely traverse down the path of sexual immorality because we have no willingness to resist our primal desires. And when the consequences of our sin threatens to deprive us of further hedonistic pleasure, we obliterate anything that stands in our way...even if that is our own child.

Mother Teresa affirmed the evil nature of such an ultimate rejection of personal responsibility by declaring,

> *"It is a poverty to decide that a child must*

die so that you may live as you wish. "[33]

What can be said about a society that now brashly describes as the "moral choice" what she accurately called a "poverty?" Scripture warns,

> *"Woe to those who call evil good and good evil, who put darkness for light and light for darkness, who put bitter for sweet and sweet for bitter...their root shall be as rottenness, and their blossom shall go up as dust."* [34]

That is precisely what is happening in the United States. And if you pay attention, you can see the root of our freedom disintegrating and the blossom of our prosperity evaporating.

If we want to strike a blow for a culture of life in America, Christians must begin by doing the heavy lifting of addressing culturally our people's glaringly hedonistic and self-serving obsessions. Abortion, euthanasia, suicide, and violence are merely the logical manifestations of it.

8

THE STATE OF THE CULTURE

I was standing backstage at a conference when I first saw the video clip from CBS evening news being played as part of a different speaker's presentation. The clip began with a snowy candlelight vigil being held in the Colorado town of Boulder. In hushed tones the reporter spoke over the soft voices of residents singing "We Shall Overcome," as he recounted the loss of one of the community's dearest members:

> *"They came to celebrate a friend with candles and song. Tuesday his life came to an end."*

The video then cut to an older gentleman, a grieving resident of the town, choking back emotion as he shared,

> *"I cried. Outrage. Um, I lost a very dear friend."*

And then it happened. The camera cut to a photo of a local police officer posing with a dead elk. The reporter went on:

> *"A Boulder police officer shot the Bull Elk, known by many names: Big Boy, George, and Elmo."*

As I was fighting back the urge to laugh, a woman was interviewed in the clip whose words sucked the air right out of the room:

> *"And I don't see a whole lot of difference between the shooting of this defenseless Elk and the shooting of schoolchildren in Connecticut."*

A gasp went through the audience. As the clip came to a close, that same woman was seen holding up a candle, singing the words of "Amazing Grace."

Let that sink in. Let what she said sink in. She finds moral equivalence between a soulless creature being shot dead and those precious souls of Sandy Hook Elementary

School being gunned down in their first grade classrooms.

What can account for that kind of offensive witlessness? I remember sitting there at that conference dumbfounded after the clip was played. I can't even remember anything that the speaker went on to say because I was just fixated on the staggering foolishness embodied in such a perspective.

But if we're honest, that is precisely the mentality that increasingly surrounds us. Many of you may still remember a young woman named Brittany Maynard. Brittany was a 29-year-old newlywed, trying for a child, who was unexpectedly diagnosed with glioblastoma, a very aggressive form of brain cancer.

After considering the various forms of treatment available to her, as well as their potential side effects and ultimate futility, Maynard decided against seeking conventional care. She also became overly fearful of the potential ineffectiveness of palliative care at home and decided her best option was suicide.

And so, Maynard spent the last few months of her life relocating to Oregon where she could be prescribed life-ending drugs, and then speaking out as an advocate for legalized suicide.

There is no doubt that Brittany's story was tragic, and under normal circumstances most anyone would agree that such extraordinarily personal trauma should not be a matter of public discussion and debate.

But it became controversial because Maynard chose herself to interject her suffering as a way to publicly promote and advocate suicide as a form of compassionate care, all while bizarrely maintaining her contention that killing herself with drugs was not suicide.

She famously opined for CNN,

"I've had the medication for weeks. I am not suicidal. If I were, I would have consumed that medication long ago. I do not want to die. But I am dying. And I want to die on my own terms."[35]

These self-contradictory, depressing, and ultimately dangerous words became a rallying cry for far too many in our culture. And what was most alarming had to be the number of supposedly God-fearing believers who championed Maynard as not just a catalyst for change, but a courageous hero.

Why is it so alarming? Because her entire line of thinking rests in humanist ideology and is an affront to Biblical thinking. Yet supposed Bible believers were championing it.

First of all, "dying on your own terms" is what *every* person committing suicide – whether with a gun, a rope, a bridge, or a bottle of pills – at least claims to be doing. It is intellectually incongruent to allege you are not suicidal all while you possess the weapon you will use as you wait for the perfect time to kill yourself.

Secondly, "dying on your own terms" is not heroic or courageous. It is everything the opposite of those things. Putting yourself to sleep like a dog cheapens the sanctity of human life, assuming it has no value or purpose beyond that of mere beasts.

Thirdly, Christians will be mindful of the truth Paul teaches in his first letter to the church at Corinth that our lives are not our own to begin with. Job reminds us that it is not up to man to number his days – that such authority belongs to the One to whom *we* belong and the one to whom we owe our existence.

And finally, only a culture that produces individuals who equate elk killing to the murder of children can find courage in an act of cowardice. I know that sounds harsh and I don't mean to be lacking in sympathy for the family of Brittany Maynard. But we all recognize suicide as an extraordinarily selfish act, and what Brittany committed was unquestionably suicide. Taking pills to kill yourself is not facing your final days with courage. It is avoiding your final days. There's a big difference.

I say that as one who has watched several individuals diagnosed with the very same condition of glioblastoma put their lives in God's hands and say, "Father, I don't know why I have to go through this or what you're possibly going to do to be glorified through it. But I am content to give you control, and to commit every moment there is still breath in my lungs to singing your praise and testifying to your greatness."

That is courage.

The idea that a life of pain, difficulty, or seemingly insurmountable challenge is not worth living has profound consequences not just on those facing devastating diagnoses or reaching the twilight of their earthly lives. It also leads to frightening phenomena at the other end of life's spectrum, like what we are witnessing with the emergence of "wrongful birth" lawsuits.

In case you're fortunately unfamiliar with this appalling spectacle, a wrongful birth lawsuit is one where the parents of a severely handicapped (physically or mentally) sues the obstetrician or medical personnel who failed to notify them during the pregnancy that they would be giving birth to such an imperfect child.

The legal argument goes that had the

doctor properly informed the parents of their unborn child's condition, the parents would have had the child killed and simply tried again. As I read about wrongful birth cases like those of Jade Fields or Ryan Powers I wonder what it must be like to find out that your parents sued your birth doctor because he didn't tip them off to how imperfect you are so that they could kill you.

It's astounding that anyone thinks this way. It's even more astounding that our society has become so debased, so backwards that those who think this way are financially rewarded for it.

But that is the culture that surrounds us. That is the culture where God has placed us. That is the culture where we have been sent as missionaries, like Jonah to Nineveh, to preach repentance and the truth of a better way. As you may recall, Jonah decided Nineveh wasn't worth his time, ran away from God's command, and spent three days sitting in the belly of a massive fish thinking about his disobedience.

8. The State of the Culture

Whether or not you live by water, perhaps we'd all be wise to learn from his mistake.

9

WHY ARE WE SURPRISED?

I was nearing the end of my sophomore year in college on April 20, 1999. As I walked past the dorm lounge, I noticed a large number of guys standing there in silence, watching the big screen TV. I walked in to see images of young people running across a school campus with their hands on their heads as though they were in a military camp.

SWAT teams dressed all in black, police crime scene tape, teenagers being loaded onto stretchers – just 8 years before the Virginia Tech University massacre, and 13 years before the horror at Sandy Hook Elementary, I watched live as the tragedy of the Columbine massacre unfolded before my eyes.

As a future teacher, I remember being pretty fixated on the aftermath of this famous schoolhouse slaughter. I watched so many interviews with victims, witnesses, parents and friends of those involved.

But nothing stood out to me more in those days than the analyses and explanations provided by the media and their experts. These were the people that we were trusting to tell us why two high school teenagers would ever perpetrate such a violent act. We were turning to them to explain what could cause behavior like this, and ultimately what could stop it.

And there, sitting behind their half-glasses with mountains of sociological survey data, and speaking to media elites, they espoused the commonly accepted culprits: Eric Harris and Dylan Klebold were motivated by violent video games and movies. They were ostracized at school without many friends. They suffered from Attention Deficit Disorder and other medical conditions. And that was it. Those were the answers we were supposed to accept. And amazingly, such sophistry, such unimaginative and painfully inadequate conclusions received the stamp of approval from our culture.

The country's Vice President at the time, Al Gore, had been called upon to give the eulogy for the slain. In it he seemed to concur with these confused voices as he stated,

> *"If you are a parent, your children need your attention...We must have the courage not to look away from those who feel despised and rejected...Children look to us...We must protect them from the violence and cruelty in our popular culture...It is too easy for a young child to get a gun...We need to look for the earliest signs of trouble -- and teach our children to resolve their differences with reason and conscience, not with flashes of passion.*"[36]

Don't get me wrong, I agree with everything that Vice President Gore said. And it's crucially important to understand how those concerns he articulated can fuel aggression in those whose lives have already come off the tracks.

But the tragic reason Columbine was not the last such school shooting we've been forced to endure should tell us that our only hope of preventing them from continuing comes from curing the disease that has derailed young people like Harris and Klebold, Adam Lanza, and Seung-Hui Cho – not from merely eliminating peripheral toxins that accelerated the evil that was already festering.

Let me make it personal. When I was in high school and college, my friends and I loved to play violent video games like *James Bond GoldenEye: 007*. Rumor is that some of them (not me, of course) even skipped classes on occasion to have an all-day Bond fest. We watched violent movies as well. And not the violent movies with redeeming social value like *Saving Private Ryan*, *We Were Soldiers*, or *The Patriot*. No, we're talking Hollywood slasher movies like the Scream franchise. Consider also that with a Dad in the U.S. Air Force, my family moved frequently. Having friends wasn't always a luxury for me – so much so that I invented them (Clarice the Mule, based off the movie *The Apple Dumpling Gang Rides Again*, was my imaginary friend until I was in the 5th grade). And when it comes to Attention Deficit Disorder, the only reason I wasn't diagnosed with it as a child was because it wasn't in existence then.

Why does any of this matter? Because despite possessing each of these "causes of Columbine," and despite the ease with which I could have accessed weapons, I never once even thought about killing myself or my classmates. Does that reality mean that those movies and video games are edifying and appropriate? Of course not. But what it means is that they fall woefully short in explaining the root cause of the Columbine massacre.

In his memorial speech, Gore challenged,

> *"In a culture rife with violence – where too many young people place too little value on a human life – we can rise up and say no more."*[37]

9. Why Are We Surprised?

Indeed we can, if we are willing. Are we? Unfortunately, all signs indicate that our culture remains content to accept benign explanations that only begin to scratch at the surface of the dilemmas we face, so long as those explanations are offered by someone with a degree from an approved institution and are bathed in shallow rhetoric that tickles itching ears. Any appeal to moral authority, personal responsibility, and eternal expectation is to be expelled from our airwaves, our courtrooms, and lecture halls. And thus, the fairly self-evident understanding of what is happening to us evades the conscience of our people.

After all, only a culture starved of truth fails to grasp that the tragedies unfolding daily in our schools, our homes, and on our streets are the direct result of an intentional deprivation of moral grounding.

- When we teach young people from their first day in high school biology class that human life is nothing but a cosmic accident with no ultimate value, destiny, or purpose...

- When we teach young people that their existence is nothing but the worthless conglomeration of molecules that came together purely by chance billions of years ago...

- When we teach young people that upon death their existence merely ceases, becomes worm food, and ends without any sense of eternal justice...

- When we teach young people that murdering an infant is a choice...

- When we teach young people that killing off the unwanted elderly is humane...

- When we teach young people that suicide is acceptable if it's assisted by a physician, and in some cases like those of glioblastoma it is courageous and honorable...

- When we teach young people that eliminating the sick and the terminal is ethical and justifiable...

9. Why Are We Surprised?

When we teach them such things, we have successfully ingrained into the minds of an entire generation that life itself is worthless. How then can it be surprising when those same young people treat life as though it is worthless?

Do you see how desperately a new voice, a wiser voice, *our* voice is needed?

How do we make a difference? How do we engage this battle? This is how: our society is asking the questions and those of us who are pro-life need to be providing them the answers. They want to know why our kids aren't acting right, and we must tell them it's because we spend all day, every day, teaching them that there is no such thing as "right."

They, as Mr. Gore pondered, want to know why "too many young people place too little value on a human life," and we must tell them it's because we spend all day, every day, reinforcing the lie that life has no value.

We will be successful in transforming our culture when we begin convincing them that the bad fruit we are reaping is the direct result of the bad seeds we are planting. And the best way to get better fruit? Try a new seed.

10

WHAT IT IS, NOT WHAT IT DOES

Of course, it's not just planting *any* new seed. It's planting the right one that matters. So how do we convince the culture that we've got it? The same way you convince anyone of anything. Evidence.

We explain the foundation and we demonstrate the result.

As we've demonstrated, post-modern society (perhaps better defined as the post-Christian West) rejects the uniqueness and sacredness of human life. What used to be a foundational pillar of our civilization has gone by the wayside in light of modern man's almost strictly utilitarian view of human existence.

That's a fancy term, but all it means is that the culture we live in has come to value human life for what it can do for the rest of us. Even well-intentioned pro-lifers fall into this mindset. You can observe it when you hear them argue against abortion while saying things like, "You might be aborting the person who discovers the cure to cancer!" or "You could be aborting the next Einstein, Edison, Beethoven, or Bach!"

From a Godly, pro-life perspective, one that values the *intrinsic* worth of humanity, it doesn't matter who you are aborting – it's equally tragic. Highlighting people who have done impressive things for humanity only reinforces the lie that life must *merit* its worth. That stands in stark contrast with the eternal truth written all over the pages of God's Word.

Take the Apostle Paul, giving what may be the greatest stump speech in history, standing before the Greeks at the meeting of the Areopagus, and proclaiming:

> *"And He made from one man*
> *every nation of mankind to live on*
> *all the face of the earth, having*

*determined their appointed times
and the boundaries of their
habitation.* "[38]

This significant truth is what gives
believers the basic understanding that there
is something unique and sacred about every
human life. It's what tells us that
Beethoven's and Bach's lives were not
worthy of protection simply because they
contributed great music to our civilization,
that Einstein's and Edison's lives were not
worthy of protection simply because of
their contributions to science.

Life is not valuable for what it does; life
is valuable for what it is – a being made in
the image of Almighty God. Sure that's true
for Einstein and Bach, but it's equally true
for that little Down syndrome baby now
targeted for extinction by a sick society that
has all but totally rejected divine truth.

Just consider what happens in the
government school system every year. As
students – churched and un-churched – fill
biology and science classes, they are taught
this one, fundamental, primary point about
life: it is a total accident. Far from

remaining neutral on the question of human origin, the government has embraced a state religion of humanism, and has proactively legislated that tax dollars will be used to cram it down the throats of every child.

Kids are taught that it is scientific fact that human beings are nothing more than the product of mind-numbingly impossible cosmic chance. It would be comical if it wasn't so tragic. Admittedly I have always found it quite humorous when atheist social commentators like Bill Maher or Richard Dawkins incessantly scoff at the Creation account of Genesis, with its mystical gardens and talking snakes, for being irrational. I always want to ask those that mock the impracticality of the Biblical account if they have ever paused to consider that their alternative story is an even taller tale:

> All the (potential) matter in the universe was at one moment in the finite past confined to a tiny pinpoint of light that, inexplicably, without provocation, rhyme or reason, one day decided to become aggressively agitated and expand at an unimaginably, miraculous, enigmatically

rapid rate.

This, we are told, set into motion a series of extraordinary events that included piles of dead, inorganic material spontaneously popping to life, violating all known laws of science. Once alive, it assembled itself into a living ball of goo, that eventually tired of being just goo (who wouldn't?) and popped out legs.

A few millennia later, this goo-with-legs decided to grow some feathers and take to the air. After tiring of flight, the creature flopped down to earth, grew massive amounts of hair, hunched over, walked around as a monkey for a few thousand years until it later stumbled across a razor, shaved, and became human. Author Frank Peretti accurately calls it, "Goo to you by way of the zoo."

Why Christians ever feel intellectually inferior to grown adults who profess faith in such a remarkable fantasy is beyond me. Particularly since our unwillingness to confront this silly storyline of human origin is resulting in deadly consequences. After all, there's a reason why Eric Harris wrote in his journal just before committing the

Columbine murders, "NATURAL SELECTION. F---ers should be shot,"[39] and wore a t-shirt under his trench coat the day of the slaughter with the words "Natural Selection" printed in bold.[40]

When you have systematically organized an educational program that intellectually strips humanity of its eternal purpose and significance, no number of self-esteem classes will replace what we have destroyed. Having convinced kids that there is no Creator who holds the answers to mankind's curious existence, we idiotically counsel their natural bewilderment by telling them to "look within themselves" to find ultimate meaning.

But of course, they aren't God. And so, when they can't find the answers within themselves, many of them just choose to end their existence. And even those who don't have still been poisoned with a lethal lie that, when it fully manifests, will eventually destroy both them and the culture they have grown to define. The society they inherit comes to view life as nothing but a mere product or machine part.

This is the materialist, collectivist, socialist view of human worth: that there is nothing valuable about any one individual. There's no divine spark of God's unique craftsmanship inherent in every created being. Rather, man is regarded as a mere piece to fit into a larger puzzle, an individual part that functions within a larger engine.

For the purposes of full disclosure, I am admittedly missing that male testosterone chip that makes me really understand and appreciate automobiles. As long as it's running and gets me where I need to go, that's good enough for me.

Still, I know enough to know that an engine is made up of several working parts that must all be completing their designed function sufficiently for the engine to operate properly. This is the view of humanity's worth that we are coming to embrace in the United States. While there is nothing special about any one individual, we find our worth in serving the collective. That's the philosophy being bred in schools across America, and being reinforced by pop culture at every turn. So why is it a problem? Why is Biblical Christianity better?

Simply ask yourself what happens when a certain engine part – say, a piston – breaks its connecting rod and no longer functions the way it was supposed to? When that happens we normally take our engine to the mechanic, and if he can't fix it, we throw that piston away and replace it. Once the piece is no longer doing its job, it is of no use to us. And if it's not discarded in a timely manner, it can become a real drag on the effective operation of the engine.

As this utilitarian, materialistic philosophy has taken root in the United States, we now witness our society treating human life in the exact same manner of a piston. When a certain part is no longer serving us or functioning as originally designed, we take it to the doctor. If he can't fix it, we discard that individual because they aren't serving the collective, and their continued presence becomes a drain on our resources. This is the logical basis for abortion, infanticide, euthanasia, doctor-assisted suicide, and every other life-destroying practice we are seeing explode with frightening regularity in our culture.

But the Apostle Paul is providing us the better way. It's the Christian alternative view that teaches individual worth actually has nothing to do with self. In fact, the foundation of an individual's value comes from the fact that he was made for a purpose, designed by a Creator who knew everything about him, and who formed him in His very own image. The significance of that point and the power it wields to change hearts and minds cannot be overstated.

Just before Christmas this year I was perusing my Twitter feed and came across evidence for this very truth from the most unlikely source. Here's the powerful personal account of a man I've never met, but whose testimony affirms the truth I know well (I've edited only a few grammatical mistakes and the curse words):

"I was about 22, I mostly lived to party. I'd get drunk every single night at my favorite dive bar before heading downtown to whatever party or bar was happening. I had nothing going for me. Dead end job, lived with my parents, barely working car. I probably would have wrapped it around a tree drunk if given a few more years.

On my birthday, a bunch of my friends came out, and I got exceedingly drunk. I ran into an old fling, nice enough girl. We had a one night stand. A few months later, I'm working the night shift stocking shelves at a grocery store, I get a call. It's the girl from my birthday night. She's pregnant.

F***. I make $9.50 an hour and live at home. What the h*** am I supposed to do? Call a guy I know who is a pastor. He's a pretty understanding dude. Asks me what I plan to do. Plan? I *haven't planned a thing in my life, I live in the moment. He asks me if I want a kid. "H*** no!" He gives me a card, says it's a relationship counselor, tells me to call her and explain my situation.*

I called her, explained what was going on, and she had a reasonable proposal: why don't you two come meet me, and we can talk about this in an environment that feels safe and open. I call Jenna (my wife now). I tell her that I want to try to be a good person and maybe we could talk about it with this person who is an expert in bad situations.

First meeting comes and this lady is a little out there, but very understanding. Jenna and I are able to talk about what we want. We come to a tentative agreement that we should get to know each other. Jenna's dad is a doctor, she's had everything she's ever wanted or needed in life. She's a great student and college athlete. I'm a f*** up, my parents, while *wealthy, have mostly cut me off and I have an awful relationship with them at this time.*

*That poor woman is faced with a couple bad choices: hitch her wagon to a f****** deadbeat loser, get an abortion, give the baby up for adoption or keep the baby, cut me off and try to finish school as a single mom at 20. In the worst decision (later best) she's ever made, she decided to go with me...a guy who stocks grocery stores, living in his parents basement with a car that barely runs.*

We started going to couples counseling twice a week, literally to get to know each other. Now Jenna had never dated anyone before. Suddenly this deadbeat scruffball shows up with her at all her family events, church and dinner on Sunday, the whole 9 yards.

We eventually got to the point where we decided we wanted to keep the baby and maybe get married. This is about 4-5 months into the pregnancy. She hadn't told her parents yet and she was starting to show a little. Everytime we tried to tell them, she'd have a panic attack and we wouldn't tell them. Eventually it got to the point where someone had to tell them or they would guess. Eventually I realized that I was going to have to tell them myself. I looked her dad up on his hospital's website and called his office. Asked to meet with him.

*Folks, I was not a brave man. I always took the easy way, I was a coward and a weasel. But I went to that f****** meeting and I broke that poor man's heart. He knew what I was, and now his beautiful, intelligent, sweet daughter was forever linked to me. Hardest thing I've ever done is telling a good man that I may have just ruined his daughter's dreams, and his dreams for her.*

My Father-in-law is a saint folks. He took it stoically. He didn't yell *or scream or kick my a**. He thanked me for telling him and said he would be in touch, that he had to talk to his family. Jenna called me an hour later. She was furious. Called me every name in the book and then some. Her mom called an hour later and asked me to come to dinner that night. Talk about walking into a bad situation. I went that night.*

It went great actually. Her family was supportive of her, wanted to make the best of the situation and offered to pay for the counseling we were going to (100 bucks a week is a lot when you make $9.50). After a month or two we decided we would get married. Jenna dropped out of school and started sewing decorative pillows to make a little money. I started to get my act together with work. I went from a s*** employee to the best mother****** they had.

I completely turned my life around. I had no choice, it was sink or swim and I had to carry two others on my back. I worked my tail off and got some promotions and small raises. Out of the blue, my parents made us an astounding offer: they would buy a very modest house for us, and would defer payments for the first couple years of our marriage.

We found a nice house in a safe neighborhood and they bought it. A month later Charlie was born. Charlie changed my world. From the moment I found out about him, he began to save me. Charlie transformed me from a directionless f*** up to a man with a purpose. Hindsight is great right? I didn't see it then, but that tiny little human inside Jenna changed me more than any outside influence ever could. He made me be a man, he saved my life, and be brought the love of my life into my life.

So why am I pro life? Because I understand that a small, seemingly insignificant and helpless human can have a profound impact on the world. Simply by existing an unborn child has the power to save someone, to radically change a life. And Charlie didn't just save me, he brought Jenna and I together, and through that came Henry and Annie, two more wonderful amazing people who will have a huge impact on their world.

A life is never a mistake! The power in a life to save others is immense. It may not be clear at the time, but in time it becomes clear. Charlie saved my life. I would never want someone to lose that amazing chance.[41]

This is the significance, the indescribable worth, inherent in every human being regardless of the circumstances of their conception.

Dating back to the days immediately following the Great Flood, God made very clear that man was set above all living things. In the covenant with Noah, God put the most severe punishment in place for anyone who would destroy the life of a human being.[42] Why? Because that human being could do neat things? No. Because that human being is wanted and appreciated? No. Because that human being contributes admirably to the collective? No. But because that human being – all human beings – are made in God's image.

Imagine for a second what would happen if we started teaching kids that profound truth: that despite all your circumstances, difficulties, disabilities, or struggles, you are made in the image of the Almighty who has a distinct plan and purpose for your life.

And even when you feel the emptiest, remember that your life was worth the Creator's time in forming you and fitting you with an eternal destiny. You don't feel like you "fit" in this life? Recognize that you must fit perfectly into God's eternal architecture or you wouldn't be here.

This is transformative stuff. It would spark a revolutionary reframing of our culture from the bottom up. And remember what we established earlier: politicians follow the masses. You want laws to change relative to suicide, euthanasia, abortion, and infanticide? This is how it will happen. Not by finding an effective political leader who will impose righteousness on the people, but by transforming a people to righteousness, who will then demand it in their leaders.

You and I, surrendered as vessels to convey God's truth unapologetically in every area of our culture where He wisely places us, are the only ones who can make that happen.

11

SO WHAT SHOULD YOU DO?

So how is the best way for you to do it? How can you most effectively teach truth – particularly about life – to our culture? What are the best practices, the best approaches, the best tactics? How about this for an answer: *I don't know.*

I know you're annoyed right now, but allow me to explain that non-answer before you spike the book and walk away thinking I've ripped you off. I don't know how *you* can best do it – because I don't know you. I do know how *I* can best do it, and maybe that's a start?

As I mentioned earlier, God has positioned me in a public high school classroom. So the way I teach the culture is in my witness to those students I get every year. I do it through the newspaper column I write occasionally, and the online commentaries I author daily. I do it through the videos I create and send out regularly to my mailing list. I do it through speaking engagements, pulpit-filling opportunities, and through books like this.

In other words, I've tried to find the areas in my life where God has gifted me and I use those gifts and talents to do His important work. If Jesus revolutionized the whole world through just a handful of ordinary, unimpressive guys committed to that concept, imagine what He could do if all those who say they are His followers today committed to the same? Or even if just the people that read this book did it? So can He count on you?

This is usually the time when people tell me that they just don't have the same gifts that I do. Well of course you don't! God wouldn't be a very smart chess player if He loaded His team up with a bunch of bishops but no rooks, now would He?

11. So What Should You Do?

We've all been gifted differently, and if you don't know your gifts (and honestly most people do, but are simply afraid of looking conceited if they acknowledge them as gifts), at least ask someone close to you. Chances are they won't have any problem telling you because it's obvious.

Some of you can write amazingly well. What are you using that gift to accomplish? Are you writing for newspapers, blogs, newsletters, Facebook posts, sharing the truth about life and its inherent value and purpose? Have you considered writing a weekly encouragement handout and making them available at your church or on the tables of waiting rooms and coffee shops? If not, why not?

Some of you can speak confidently and articulately. What are you using that gift to accomplish? Are you teaching Sunday School classes, creating video commentaries to post on social media addressing important issues? They don't have to be fancy, and they shouldn't be long. Short, inspirational, truth-filled messages that even if only your small group of Facebook friends see, may still get shared and impact someone you never even knew.

I've mentioned social media a couple times now – if you have that ability and gift to connect with people through it, are you using it as a gift meant for God's glory and the propagation of His truth? Are you finding and sharing meaningful material? Are you promoting Godliness and thoughtful, life-affirming material through your efforts? The power of social media is immense. Consider that a man was elected to the White House in this country in large part because of his ability to use social media to completely bypass the filter of standard, mass media. Whether you like him or not is immaterial. It shows the power at your fingertips if you use it or can learn it.

How about this one – can you pray? Do you have a spiritual gift of leading prayer for and with others? Have you considered finding people with similar gifts, and with a similar time and devotion to its power, and coordinating weekly prayer meetings, or daily prayer times?

11. So What Should You Do?

Do you have the gift of organization? If so, what are you doing with it? Have you volunteered to help crisis pregnancy centers with their bookkeeping? What about organizing church functions to reach out to your community on the value of every life? Have you organized a mentorship program with the local elementary school where Godly people can begin meeting regularly with young, impressionable children and teaching them things of value – particularly about the gift of life?

Are you gifted at preaching? Do you have a congregation that you can embed these principles into every sermon you share? That isn't to say that abortion or suicide needs to come up as a topic in every message you write. It is to say that life-affirming encouragement, Godly principles about the value inherent in life can and should.

Are you gifted at automobile repair? I'm serious. Are you mechanically minded? Do you think that gift can't be used for good?

I met a family at a speaking engagement

a couple years ago who were members of that church for one reason. They had been a struggling family dealing with unemployment and hunger. Their one vehicle was having problems and they took it to the local mechanic they knew. The mechanic discovered that they had a serious issue that was going to be very expensive to fix. The family was at a loss – they had no money, no hope of getting any money, and nowhere to turn. That mechanic made them a deal – "I fix your car and my bill to you is that you and your whole family come with me to church every Sunday next month." Incredible.

That was two years ago. The family still attends and are now Christians. Don't tell me your mechanical gifts can't be used to glorify God and teach His principles.

Are you relentlessly energetic? Are you the kind of person that no one understands where your drive comes from and why it never seems to stop? Where are you volunteering? Where are you investing it?

Have you been gifted with money?

11. So What Should You Do?

Some of you have been. Some of you have great jobs that pay you far more than you need to live on. So what are you doing with it?

You know as well as I do that everyone spends the money we have. When Jenny and I were first married we were living paycheck to paycheck. When we had our first kid, I made more money than we had as newlyweds, but we were still living paycheck to paycheck. We have three kids now and had we not started disciplining our finances, the temptation to spend all we make and live paycheck to paycheck would remain immense.

So it simply stands to reason that the people making fifteen times what I make are facing the same pressure and temptation – spend all they make. If you have financial blessing, God has given that to you for you to bless others with it. Are you?

Maybe you don't have the ability to speak like some pro-life speaker you just were inspired by. But you do have the ability to invest in his or her ministry and help them promote that message of truth.

Maybe you can't write like someone whose book you just picked up (no, I'm not talking about me, I promise) but you can help them distribute it widely with an investment.

Maybe you don't have the time to go down and change linens and stock shelves at the crisis pregnancy center, but you can write them a check to pay someone who does. Don't think it makes a difference?

For years, Boise's Planned Parenthood sat undisturbed and unchallenged in a quiet northern neighborhood. But in October, 2011, a new kid showed up on the block and presented a very big challenge. The loud and proud pro-life Stanton Health Care Clinic moved in right next door to Planned Parenthood, posting big signs offering free pregnancy tests, ultrasounds and other services that Planned Parenthood charges for.

"The strategic location we believe is key," Stanton founder Brandi Swindell said. "We want to get as close as possible to abortion-

providers, specifically Planned Parenthood, so that girls truly have a choice."...

All this meant the world to single, 19-year-old Pattie, who asked not to have her last name used, last December when she took a home pregnancy test and discovered she might be pregnant. She and her mother, residents of the Treasure Valley in which Boise sits, headed right for Planned Parenthood to get an ultrasound verification. But Pattie ended up in tears there as Planned Parenthood demanded $150 for the ultrasound, money she just didn't have...

Moments later, Pattie's mother, despairing about her daughter's predicament inside Planned Parenthood, saw the signs for free ultrasounds next door at Stanton...

Pattie and her mom left Planned Parenthood for Stanton and immediately felt a difference. "I got like three hugs the minute I came in here," Pattie said. "They were just so happy to see me."

"That's the Holy Spirit," Swindell insisted. "That's the body of believers, the pro-life community coming together and actually showing love to these women." Since then,

Pattie's received so much care and free stuff for her coming baby, she can hardly wait for her Stanton visits. "[43]

Do you know how the Stanton Clinic got built? Christians with money decided to invest it in something meaningful. This is how you save lives. This is how you change a culture.

Because remember, at 19 years old, Pattie has friends. Pattie's friends are going to hear about the Stanton Clinic – they may even go with her and see for themselves. Those friends may have other friends who are in similar situations as Pattie, and as a consequence of Christians using the money they'd been blessed with to build and staff a facility like Stanton, those lives may be saved too. And Planned Parenthood in Boise will shut its doors not because a single law changed or our lawmakers ever showed courage. It will close due to lack of business.

This was the whole point of Jesus' Parable of the Talents. In the account, Christ tells of a wealthy landowner who left for a journey. But before going, he called in three of his servants, entrusting each of them with a little bit of his wealth. He gave the first five talents (an amount of gold), the second received two talents, and the last one was given one talent.

When the wealthy man returned from his trip, he found that the first servant had invested the five talents and made five more, the second had invested the two talents and made two more, but the final servant had hidden away his talent so it would not be stolen or taken. The final servant returned to the master only what had been given to him. This angered the landowner who confiscated the talent, gave it to the first servant, and had the last one thrown out into the street.

For those who truly want to live like Jesus, it would be wise to pay attention to the fact that all of His teachings focused on building His spiritual kingdom. Go back to the parable, but recognize that you and I are the servants. And rather than an amount of gold, God has entrusted each of us with various skills, abilities, and gifts – our "talents" (although again, for some of us it might be that God has literally blessed you with financial wealth as your gift).

So what are you using those talents for? To make friends? To make peace? To be liked? To live comfortably? Or are you investing them in something that God cares about? Are you using them for something He desires and instructs – like caring for, protecting, and defending the "least of these?"

Whenever I teach my history classes about the era of the Holocaust, I never stop thinking about what exactly the German churches were doing in that deadly environment. Where was the opposition? Where were the pulpits flaming with righteous indignation, Godly rebuke, and unwavering condemnation of what was happening in their culture? There were thousands of Christian ministers in Germany at the time, and yet history only remembers two of them: Martin Niemoller and Dietrich Bonhoeffer. History remembers the names of the two who stood for righteousness and against the evil of their age.

11. So What Should You Do?

The same is true of Biblical history. The twelve spies who went to scout the land of Canaan before Israel's invasion saw ten come back with discouraging reports. Can you name them? Can you name even one of them? Probably not. History remembers the two, Caleb and Joshua, who stood for faith and against the disobedient voices of their age.

And it's true in our American history as well. Sometimes at speaking engagements when this topic comes up I will ask the audience to raise their hands if they know the names Pierce or Buchanan. To make sure they're honest and not just trying to appear smart, I warn them that I am likely to call on them to tell everyone who those individuals are or were. I think in all the times I've asked that question I've had less than five people raise their hands. To make my point, I then ask for a show of hands of those who know the name Lincoln. You can imagine the response.

Pierce and Buchanan were the two presidents who preceded Abraham Lincoln into office and served almost identical lengths of time in the White House. They dealt with the same national crisis over the same great moral question of that day. Yet both Pierce and Buchanan chose to compromise. They chose to turn away, to try to cover over and disregard what Lincoln refused to ignore. And history remembers fondly the one who rejected conformity and compromise, who stood for justice and virtue regardless the cost.

God is asking you to do the same this day. What is your choice? This is your defining moment.

CITATIONS

[1] "Iceland is on pace to virtually eliminate Down syndrome through abortion," August 14, 2017. Published online: https://twitter.com/cbsnews/status/89725404217 8650113?lang=en.

[2] Quinones, Julian and Arijeta Lajka, "What kind of society do you want to live in? Inside the country where Down syndrome is disappearing," August 14, 2017. Published online: https://www.cbsnews.com/news/down-syndrome-iceland/?linkId=40953194.

[3] Biden, Joe. "October 11, 2012 Debate Transcript," Commission on Presidential Debates. Published online: http://www.debates.org/index.php?page=october-

11-2012-the-biden-romney-vice-presidential-debate.

[4] Gehrke, Joel. "Joe Biden: 'Abortion is Always Wrong,'" National Review, September 22, 2015. Published online: http://www.nationalreview.com/article/424463/joe-biden-abortion-always-wrong-joel-gehrke.

[5] "Meet the Press," NBC News, August 17, 2008.

[6] U.S. Supreme Court, Oral Arguments in *Roe v. Wade*, 410 U.S. 113 (1973). Reprinted online: http://www.oyez.org/cases/1970-1979/1971/1971_70_18/reargument.

[7] *Roe v. Wade*, 410 U.S. 113 (1973).

[8] Ibid.

[9] Tribe, Laurence. *Harvard Law Review*, 1973.

[10] Lazarus, Edward. *The Lingering Problems With Roe v. Wade*, 2002. Reprinted at www.FindLaw.com.

[11] Subcommittee on Separation of Powers to Senate Judiciary Committee S-158, Report, 97th Congress, 1st Session, 1981. Find more quotations and testimony at http://www.abort73.com/index.php?/abortion/medical_testimony.

[12] Ibid.

[13] Ibid.

[14] PersonhoodUSA. "Video: Planned Parenthood Declares War on Science," Oct. 26, 2010, printed online: http://www.personhoodusa.com/blog/video-

planned-parenthood-declares-war-science. Full
debate posted online:
http://eternityimpact.blogspot.com/2010/10/deba
te-video.html.
[15] Ibid.
[16] Ibid.
[17] Ibid.
[18] *Planned Parenthood of Southeastern
Pennsylvania v. Casey*, 505 U.S. 833 (1992).
[19] Bork, Robert. Slouching Towards Gomorrah:
Modern Liberalism and American Decline (New
York: Regan Books, HarperCollins, 1996, phk. ed),
111.
[20] Rosen, Jeffrey. "Worst Choice," in The New
Republic, February 24, 2003. Reprinted online:
http://www.tnr.com/article/worst-choice.
[21] Saddleback Civil Forum on the Presidency,
August 17, 2008. Transcript reprinted online:
http://transcripts.cnn.com/TRANSCRIPTS/0808/17/
se.01.html.
[22] Lincoln, Abraham. The "House Divided Against
Itself" Speech. Quoted in The World's Famous
Orations, America: II (1818-1865), 1906. Reprinted
online: http://www.bartleby.com/268/9/22.html.
[23] *Bob Enyart Live* radio archives, aired December
2, 2008. Debate audio online:
http://kgov.com/bel/20081202.
[24] Garrison, William Lloyd. "Defense of His
Positions," 1854. Reprinted online:

http://teachingamericanhistory.org/library/index.a
sp?document=1432.

[25] Motel, Seth. "Who runs for office? A profile of
the 2%," Pew Research Center. September 3, 2017.
Published online:
http://www.pewresearch.org/fact-
tank/2014/09/03/who-runs-for-office-a-profile-of-
the-2/.

[26] Finer, Lawrence B., Lori F. Frohwirth, Lindsay A.
Dauphinee, Susheela Singh, and Ann M. Moore,
"Reasons U.S. Women Have Abortions:
Quantitative and Qualitative Perspectives,"
Perspectives on Sexual and Reproductive Health,
Volume 37, Number 3, September 2005. Pages
110-118. Published at:
http://www.guttmacher.org/pubs/journals/371100
5.pdf.

[27] Anne, Libby. "Abortion, 'God's Plan,' and 'Selfish'
Women," Patheos, February 7, 2012. Published at:
http://www.patheos.com/blogs/lovejoyfeminism/2
012/02/abortion-gods-plan-and-selfish-
women.html.

[28] Ibid.

[29] Ibid.

[30] King, Carol. "10 Worst Abortion Myths – and
How to Refute Them," Ms. Magazine, April 23,
2010. Published at:
http://msmagazine.com/blog/2010/04/23/10-
worst-abortion-myths-and-how-to-refute-them/.

[31] Girn, Ramandeep. "Defending the Selfish Choice: Abortion Rights and the Morality of Egoism," The Undercurrent, September 2, 2006. Published at: http://theundercurrent.org/defending-the-selfish-choice-abortion-rights-and-the-morality-of-egoism/.

[32] Ibid.

[33] Downs, Rebecca. "Abortion as the Ultimate Rejection of Personal Responsibility," Live Action News, June 10, 2013. Published at: http://liveactionnews.org/abortion-as-the-ultimate-rejection-of-personal-responsibility/.

[34] The Holy Bible, Isaiah 5:20, 24 (KJV).

[35] Maynard, Brittany. "My right to death with dignity at 29," CNN, November 2, 2014. Published online: http://www.cnn.com/2014/10/07/opinion/maynard-assisted-suicide-cancer-dignity/index.html.

[36] Gore, Al. "Columbine Memorial Address," delivered April 25, 1999. Reprinted online: http://www.americanrhetoric.com/speeches/algorecolumbine.htm

[37] Ibid.

[38] The Holy Bible, Acts 17:26 (New American Standard Version)

[39] Cullen, Dave. "The Depressive and the Psychopath," Slate, April 20, 2004. Printed online: http://www.slate.com/id/2099203/

[40] Langman, Dr. Peter. "Columbine, Bullying, and the Mind of Eric Harris," Psychology Today, May 20,

2009. Printed online:
http://www.psychologytoday.com/blog/keeping-kids-safe/200905/columbine-bullying-and-the-mind-eric-harris
[41] Twitter thread available online:
https://twitter.com/NaughtyDerek/status/944043313010827266.
[42] The Holy Bible, Genesis 9:6 (New International Version)
[43] Strand, Paul. "Clinic Next Door Gets in Planned Parenthood's Face," CBN News, April 23, 2012. Published at:
http://www.cbn.com/cbnnews/healthscience/2012/April/Clinic-Next-Door-Gets-in-Planned-Parenthoods-Face/.

34886018R00080

Made in the USA
Middletown, DE
31 January 2019